SPOTLIGHT ON THE RISE AND FALL OF ANCIENT CIVILIZATIONS™

ANCIENT MESOPOTAMIAN CULTURE

BARBARA KRASNER

ROSEN
PUBLISHING

New York

Published in 2017 by The Rosen Publishing Group, Inc.
29 East 21st Street, New York, NY 10010

Copyright © 2017 by The Rosen Publishing Group, Inc.

First Edition

Library of Congress Cataloging-in-Publication Data

Names: Krasner, Barbara, author.
Title: Ancient Mesopotamian culture / Barbara Krasner.
Description: New York : Rosen Publishing, [2017] | Series: Spotlight on the rise and fall of ancient civilizations | Includes bibliographical references and index.
Identifiers: LCCN 2016001010| ISBN 9781477789032 (library bound) | ISBN 9781477789018 (pbk.) | ISBN 9781477789025 (6-pack)
Subjects: LCSH: Iraq—Civilization—To 634. | Middle East—Civilization—To 622.
Classification: LCC DS69.5 .K67 2016 | DDC 935—dc23
LC record available at http://lccn.loc.gov/2016001010

Manufactured in the United States of America

CONTENTS

MESOPOTAMIA: THE LAND BETWEEN THE RIVERS

C ivilization began in the basins of the Tigris and Euphrates Rivers. Ancient Mesopotamia covered that region. Mesopotamia means "land between the rivers." Within its boundaries, which roughly equate to present-day Iraq, lived various ethnic groups. These included Assyrians, Sumerians, and Babylonians. Each of these formed its own city-states, nations, and empires. Together, they made Mesopotamia great.

From the third to the first millennium BCE, Mesopotamia achieved major developments. Writing began about 3100 BCE. Advanced mathematics, astronomy, and music theory distinguished the civilization. But after the Persian invasion in the mid-first millennium, Mesopotamia lost its power, never to rise again.

Archaeological discoveries reveal a variety of cultural activities. Ancient texts and tablets list animals, plants, and minerals. They illustrate rituals, music and dancing, hunting, and sport.

Mesopotamia may have vanished ages ago, but its remains still give glimpses into its rich culture.

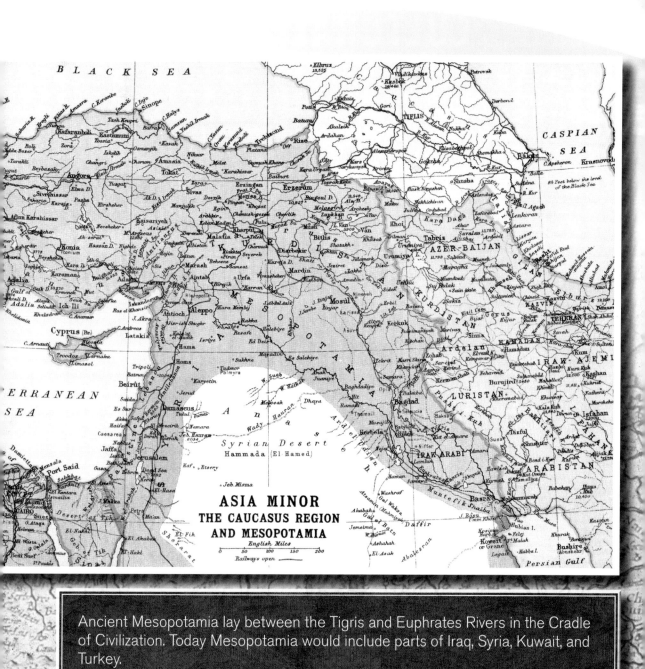

ASIA MINOR
THE CAUCASUS REGION
AND MESOPOTAMIA
English Miles
0   50   100   150   200
Railways open

Ancient Mesopotamia lay between the Tigris and Euphrates Rivers in the Cradle of Civilization. Today Mesopotamia would include parts of Iraq, Syria, Kuwait, and Turkey.

CULTURAL ICONS

Mesopotamian culture conjures up images of gods, temples, and tablets. Assyrians, Sumerians, and Babylonians worshipped a set of gods. Though these gods varied from place to place, they dictated human actions. Mesopotamians believed that people were meant to serve and please the gods. Constant prayer and worship would bring the gods' good favor.

The king was the gods' representative on Earth, so he commanded obedience and service.

King Hammurabi of Babylon took his role to heart. He ruled from 1792 to 1750 BCE. He established a code of behavior around 1750 BCE. His code was law. The Code of Hammurabi laid out punishments for crimes. It said, "Let the wronged man who has a case go before my statue called the 'King of Justice'... hear my valuable words." No one really knows if the code was used in a court of law. Kings may have applied it to make their decisions.

King Hammurabi created a set of laws governing people's behaviors. Here the king receives the laws from the god of justice. The laws became known as the Code of Hammurabi.

THE WORLD'S FIRST SYSTEM OF WRITING

Writing developed in southern Mesopotamia, in Sumer, around the eighth millennium BCE. At first people used clay tokens to count and record the number of cattle. Then they began to etch pictographs around 3500 BCE. They sharpened reeds to form styluses. For their surface, they used hardened wet clay. There was no erasing. Once the clay hardened, writing could not be changed. The clay took the form of tablets, most of which were rectangular or square. Some tablets were made from stone or metal. Writing a long text would require many tablets. They even used envelopes made from slips of clay. These safeguarded the tablets inside from damage or tampering.

Recording transactions between countries using different languages became a problem. This occurred especially when dealing with scribes who were not trained in Mesopotamia. It became necessary to simplify the form of writing to fewer signs. Scribes also simplified cuneiform.

Scribes used sharpened reeds to make impressions in clay. Cut at an angle, the reeds produced a wedge shape. This became the basis for cuneiform, Latin for "wedge."

READING, WRITING, AND ARITHMETIC

Writers were educated. They had to be, because they had to learn six hundred signs, each with multiple meanings. Most people in ancient Mesopotamia did not read or write, even priests, kings, governors, and judges. Archaeologists believe an educational system must have emerged circa 3000 BCE.

Education was a luxury only the wealthy could afford. Sometimes some orphans were adopted and sent to school, however. Students attended a school called a tablet house. The headmaster was called the expert or the father of the tablet house. A dean, or director, enforced regulations. Besides writing, students learned Sumerian, drawing, and mathematics. Students participated in memorization, dictation, writing, and lesson review. They attended school from sunrise to sunset. Learning vocabulary took intensive effort.

The educational system produced thousands of scribes. Scribes specialized in religious and royal administrations. Priests and kings dictated their letters to these professional writers.

The first writing system began in the Sumer region located in the southern part of Mesopotamia. This tablet shows the early system of pictographs using pictures and symbols.

MESOPOTAMIAN TALES

Most of what we know about Mesopotamian literature comes from the book *Babylonica*, written by a priest in the third century BCE. The literature had its roots in oral storytelling and told tales of gods and heroes. Ancient Mesopotamians preferred poetry to prose, and poets typically wrote four to twelve verses. Kings were often the subjects of historical romances. Perhaps the best-known example of Mesopotamian literature is the *Epic of Gilgamesh*. This poem tells about the deeds of an ancient king who tries to reach the plant of life so he can stay alive forever.

Besides poetry and prose, Mesopotamian literature also included hymns and prayers, riddles and proverbs, dictionaries, and grammar books. One important contribution is the Sumerian King List, which traced the line of kings from when "kingship descended from Heaven" to Hammurabi (circa 1792 BCE).

Scribes used impressions made by rolling cylinders to seal tablets. These seals showed scenes like this one from the *Epic of Gilgamesh.*

STORING THE TABLETS

The first archives in Mesopotamia consisted of tablets that chronicled tasks such as keeping inventory records. Palaces and temples often had whole rooms dedicated to archives. Sometimes tablets were kept near palace entrances for easy access for reference and record-keeping purposes. Scholars maintained their own private libraries. Scribes also had their own libraries to house their own works and that of their students. In the seventh century BCE, King Assurbanipal created the first real library in Mesopotamia at his palace in Nineveh. He could read and write and was proud of that. His many thousands of tablets each contained eight to two hundred lines.

Tablets required special handling. They were wrapped in cloth or a reed mat or placed in a jar, basket, or bag. They were stacked on wooden shelves or on mud-brick benches. Tags identified sealed contents.

King Assurbanipal 's passion for learning resulted in the creation of ancient Mesopotamia's first library at Nineveh. He collected between twenty thousand and thirty thousand cuneiform tablets.

IS THERE A DOCTOR IN THE HOUSE?

Medical professionals in ancient Mesopotamia became known as early as the third millennium BCE. People could choose from two types of healers. Medical healers were trained physicians. They mostly served royal palaces. Magical healers served in the temples. They delivered incantations to rid people of evil demons. The skill of a magical healer was passed from father to son. Little is known about the training of a medical healer. Sometimes it was difficult to tell which kind of healer a person was. Neither medical nor magical healers delivered babies. That job was performed by women who knew how to help one another give birth.

Many people believed sin caused illnesses and that demons brought on sickness. Medical healers identified symptoms and diagnosed diseases. Some treatments were associated with the shape or color of disease. For example, healers treated jaundice with yellow medicine. In general, Mesopotamian medicine remained largely a matter of superstition.

Medical practitioners wrote out their prescriptions on tablets like this one written in cuneiform from the Assyrian city of Nineveh.

SIXTY AND COUNTING

Ancient Mesopotamians developed and used a numbering system based on sixty. This continues to be the basis for our division of the hour and minute into sixty units. Although they also counted by the decimal system, by tens, they used their sixty system in math.

Each of their six hundred signs bore a numerical value. There were no fractions or division. Rather, to divide, they multiplied by reciprocals. In this system, for example, the reciprocal of five was twelve, which when multiplied would yield sixty.

Mathematicians were skilled in algebra and geometry. But they did not have the vocabulary for shapes, angles, and concepts. That became the Greek contribution to mathematics.

The Mesopotamian system of weights and measures was also based on sixty. For example, a load, to be carried by a man or animal, was equal to sixty minas. A mina was equal to sixty shekels.

This Sumerian tablet with six circles down its center shows how the Mesopotamian numbering system was based on the number six.

ANIMALS, PLANTS, AND MINERALS

Ancient Mesopotamians tried to understand and organize their world. They recorded their lists of animals, plants, and minerals on tablets by the third millennium BCE. The Sumerians and Babylonians grouped animals and human body parts differently. But these lists also identified animals now extinct, such as a long-bearded ram with widely separated and curling horns. Assyrian kings created the first zoos in their capital cities. Some animals were thought to bring good or bad luck.

The Mesopotamians paid a lot of attention to plants for their healing qualities. Assyrians and Babylonians collected rare species of plants and created the first royal botanical (plant) garden.

The Mesopotamians knew and used many rare and precious stones. Babylonian and Assyrian lists of stones usually began with lapis lazuli, imported from the East. But lists also included jasper, carnelian, agate, and rock crystal. The Mesopotamians sometimes associated magical qualities with these stones.

Mesopotamians imported precious gems to make jewelry like this gold lion-headed eagle from Sumer. The eagle uses the deep blue stone lapis lazuli.

THE WORLD MAP ACCORDING TO BABYLONIA

The key to calculating land tax rates was to survey it. To carry out a survey, the land registrar used a triangle, rods of varying lengths, a rope to measure, and a peg he could drive into the ground to hold the measuring line. Shapes of land plots could also be determined. These were useful in making maps. The Mesopotamians drew and used local maps for fields, estates, and temple grounds.

But they also produced *mappa mundi*, maps of the world. Such maps placed Babylonia at the center of the world and presented a view as the Babylonians saw it. They represented Earth as a round object surrounded by the ocean.

Maps were used for building, business transactions, taxation, navigation, and military campaigns. All maps were made of hardened clay.

Aside from maps, Mesopotamians kept lists of geographic names. They included lands, cities, bodies of water, and mountains.

The Babylonians created this earliest known map of the world on a clay tablet with cuneiform writing in about 600 BCE.

STARRY NIGHTS

One of Mesopotamia's strengths was its people's knowledge of astronomy. Astronomers kept detailed records of the movements of heavenly bodies, such as the sun, moon, planets, and constellations. They recorded movement through a system of three columns or circles. Each of these represented a station of one of the three great gods: Anu, the head of the gods; Ea, the god of wisdom; or Enlil, the god of wind.

Mesopotamians based their calendar on the movement of the moon. Each month lasted twenty-nine or thirty days.

To make their observations, Mesopotamians used several tools. To measure time, they used water clocks, bowls filled with water. Mesopotamians also relied on the sundial and the shadow clock.

Related to astronomy was the practice of astrology. The Mesopotamians believed that the movement of the planets, sun, and moon reflected events on Earth. The movement could then predict good or bad omens for gods, kings, and countries.

Ancient Mesopotamians were advanced in the science of astronomy. They used tablets to record movements of the planets. This Babylonian tablet documents the movements of Jupiter.

DANCE TO THE MUSIC

Cuneiform tablets from ancient Mesopotamia provide ample examples of musical instruments, musicians, singers, dancers, and acrobats. Music played a vital role in Mesopotamian culture. Tablets indicate the use of music at religious and magic rituals, funerals, military events, and festivals in temples and palaces. Archaeology has helped to uncover the types of musical instruments used. These included stringed instruments such as the lute, harp, and lyre. The harp sounded like a guitar. The lyre sounded like a cello. They were made of wood and layered with gold, silver, copper, lapis lazuli, and mother of pearl. But silver and bone wind instruments, such as the flute, have also been discovered. Other wind instruments included trumpets. Mesopotamians played many percussion instruments. These included silver pipes, copper clappers, bronze and clay bells, rattles, and bronze cymbals.

Music played an instrumental role in ancient Mesopotamian celebrations and rituals. This scene was recovered from the royal tombs at Ur. It shows a Sumerian harpist.

Modern music theory, the mechanics of how to make music, has its roots in Mesopotamia. From about 1800 to the middle of the first millennium BCE, Mesopotamian music used seven scales.

Musicians often enjoyed high social status. The musicians themselves were sometimes used as plunder during war or exchanged as gifts between diplomats. A chief musician had the responsibility of training apprentices, including females in the royal harem. Singers also first learned their skill as apprentices.

Selling songs was a way to earn a living in Mesopotamia. It was a popular trade, but it did not bring in much money. Both religious and nonreligious songs were sold. Hymns were performed to music. They typically told stories of kings. But there were love songs, too.

Mesopotamians danced with intention. They danced to music, singing and clapping for religious reasons. For example, both men and women performed whirling dances to honor the goddess Ishtar at the annual feast. Women alone typically performed circle dances. Acrobatic dance was part of religious celebrations.

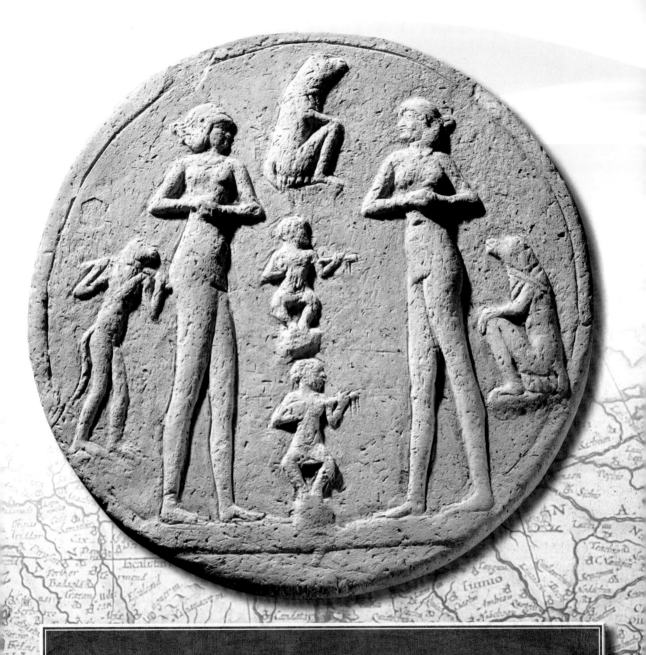

This Babylonian relief shows the importance of dancers to Mesopotamian culture. Dancing contributed to celebrations and religious rites.

ALL MESOPOTAMIA'S A STAGE

Although most Mesopotamians could neither read nor write, they could enjoy literature by attending performances. Because much of the literature was poetic, it had a built-in rhythm for chanting or singing with perhaps the lyre or harp as accompaniment.

Hymns and historical romances tended to feature kings, with good reason. Often the royal house commissioned the work, because kings too were illiterate. King Shulgi of Ur, who reigned for forty-five years from the end of the twentieth century to the beginning of the twenty-first century BCE, claimed he wrote his own compositions.

Some literary works and hymns were meant to be performed. For example, the *Epic of Gilgamesh* directly addressed members of the audience. It asked them to examine objects and buildings associated with King Gilgamesh. To perform a dialogue between two characters, two people had to participate. Religious texts were performed, too, as part of certain rituals.

King Gilgamesh is celebrated as the hero of the *Epic of Gilgamesh.* He built the walls of Aruk, shown here, nearly five thousand years ago.

HAIL TO THE GODS

Sumerian and Akkadian religion formed a common pantheon of gods. Most of the gods had both a Sumerian and Akkadian name. An was the king of the gods. He was later replaced by the Lord of the Air, Enlil, and ultimately by Marduk, the city god of Babylon. Enki or Ea in Akkadian was the god of wisdom. Ninmah was the mother of all life. Nanna or Sin was the moon and Utu or Shamash was the sun. Inanna or Ishtar was the star Venus. Her husband and the shepherd god was Dumuzi or Tammuz. Ninurta or Adad was the god of war. Myths formed around these gods.

Ancient Mesopotamians believed their purpose in life was to serve the gods. Their state of well-being, they thought, depended on their degree of worship. Temples focused on the care of gods and had religious and administrative staffs, including priests, priestesses, snake charmers, cow herders, weavers, and scribes.

This ivory plaque, thought to represent the goddess Ishtar, was found in an Assyrian palace in Nimrud. Ishtar was the goddess of love.

Many of their festivals were part of religious rituals. There was a religious relationship between the city and its god. This relationship formed the basis of some festivals, such as the New Year's Festival and the festival of each temple and its god. It was through these events that an ordinary person could communicate with a god. The New Year's Festival took place during the first eleven days of the month of Nisan, during the spring equinox. The *Epic of Creation*, the poem that told the story of how the universe was created through Marduk's victory, was performed after the first few days of prayer.

More common festivals were associated with the monthly cycle of the moon. Other festivals celebrated the shearing of sheep and thanksgiving. Individual cities had their own feasts that celebrated the delivery of first fruits and the offering of the year's first dairy products.

Some Mesopotamian festivals celebrated the shearing of sheep. This head of a female sheep, made of sandstone was probably used in rituals in the fourth century BCE.

PUT UP YOUR DUKES

In general, sports did not play a major role in Mesopotamian culture. Certain sports, however, did enjoy greater practice, as the *Epic of Gilgamesh* reveals. For example, Mesopotamian art depicts both boxing and wrestling. Men engaged in boxing wore caps and tunics. They boxed with bare hands. They may also have boxed accompanied by music. Gilgamesh wrestles a man who later becomes his best friend. Time was dedicated to wrestling competitions according to the ancient Babylonian calendar. Wrestling matches have been depicted on Mesopotamian artifacts.

Polo may also have been played. But instead of using horses, one man straddled the shoulders of another man.

Archery, like boxing and wrestling, was a combat sport, as was stick fighting. Archery, wrestling, and stick fighting were useful in war. Extensive training by coaches was necessary to prepare for it. Chariot racing has also been traced to Mesopotamia.

Foot races took place at the annual New Year's Festival.

Boxing was a popular sport as shown in this Babylonian relief from the second millennium BCE. Unlike boxers today, they wear no gloves.

THE KING'S HUNT

Hunting was a public event in Mesopotamia. Assyrian rulers hunted dangerous beasts, such as elephants and wild bulls, and ostriches. Lions were brought from Africa and kept ready for the hunt. Dogs and men with sticks waited for the lions to be let out of their cages and then they attacked. The beaters drove the beasts toward the king. From his chariot, the king used a bow or spear to kill the lion.

Hunting was popular, based on evidence from tablets and hunting scenes carved on palace walls. Royal parks housed captured animals. Hunting was not a matter of searching for food. It was a sport. Hunters used greyhounds to help. When the king's hunt proved successful, it was a political and religious victory. It meant the gods favored the king. A religious ceremony followed to celebrate. The king poured wine over the dead animals and made an offering to the gods.

Lion hunts were a favorite sport among Mesopotamian kings. This sculpted panel was found at Nineveh in the first millennium BCE.

WHAT THEY LEFT BEHIND

Persian, Greek, and Parthian invasions conquered Mesopotamian lands. By the mid-second century BCE, the ancient civilization of Mesopotamia ceased to exist. But there are aspects of Mesopotamia that remain today, such as the very act and art of writing. Literary works, such as the *Epic of Gilgamesh*, are studied and printed. The *Epic* is the oldest narrative in the world. Scientific lists laid the foundation for animal, plant, and geological classifications. Sophisticated mathematics made their way to the Greeks. Mesopotamian music theory was adopted by others.

Several times a day, the ticking of hours and minutes reminds us of an ancient civilization that measured time by using sixty as its base. Our monthly calendars recall the movement of the moon.

Archaeological discoveries have unearthed many artifacts that remind us of an unparalleled culture. These include music, singing, writing, religious rituals, celebrations, and more. The ancient Mesopotamians, whether Assyrian, Sumerian, or Babylonian, gave us much of which to be proud.

Archaeologists have uncovered many Mesopotamian artifacts showing the importance of music. This relief from the second millennium BCE shows a harp player, just one of several musicians in Mesopotamian culture.

GLOSSARY

agate A mineral with different colored bands.

Akkadian Belonging to a people living in Mesopotamia in the third millennium BCE.

archive A set of historical official papers or reports that offer knowledge about a place, establishment, or people.

Assyrian Belonging to Assyria, an early region and empire of Mesopotamia.

astrology A study of the planets, sun, and moon as they affect human behavior.

Babylonian Belonging to Babylonia, a region and empire of southern Mesopotamia.

carnelian A red gem imported from Africa and the Indus Valley.

cuneiform A system of writing that used triangles and wedges.

epic A long poem that tells a story.

ethnic Having to do with a group of people with a common tradition.

harem A group of women living in the royal palace.

incantation A group of words chanted as a magic spell or charm.

jasper A kind of crystallized stone, red in color.

lapis lazuli A deep blue mineral or gem often used in jewelry.

mappa mundi The Latin term for maps of the world.

millennium One thousand years.

pantheon Every god or goddess in a religion.

Parthian Belonging to Parthia, a country in ancient Asia that would roughly cover northern Iran today.

pictograph An early form of writing using pictures and symbols.

reciprocal In math, a relationship in which one part completes or is equal to the other.

Sumerian Belonging to Sumer, a region of southern Mesopotamia, which became Babylonia.

Ur An important Sumerian city along the Euphrates River.

FOR MORE INFORMATION

American Museum of Natural History
Central Park West at 79th Street
New York, NY 10024-5192
(212) 769-5100
Website: http://www.amnh.org
The American Museum of Natural History relates the history of Mesopotamia to nature, the environment, and science.

The California Museum of Ancient Art
P.O. Box 10515
Beverly Hills, CA 90213
(818) 762-5500
Website: http://www.cmaa-museum.org
This museum houses recovered artifacts from Assyria and Sumer. It was founded to give Southern Californians access to the roots of civilization.

The Canadian Society for Mesopotamian Studies
c/o RIM Project
University of Toronto
4 Bancroft Avenue, 4th floor
Toronto, ON M5S 1C1
Canada
(416) 978-4531
Website: http://projects.chass.utoronto.ca/csms/main.html
Founded in 1980, this society examines the literature, culture, and history of ancient Mesopotamia.

The Metropolitan Museum of Art
1000 Fifth Avenue
New York, NY 10028
(212) 535-7710
Website: http://www.metmuseum.org
The Metropolitan Museum of Art is a major center for Near Eastern art, including rock reliefs and other artifacts.

The Oriental Institute of the University of Chicago
1155 E. 58th Street
Chicago, IL 60637
(773) 702-9520
Website: https://oi.uchicago.edu
Founded in 1919, the Oriental Institute has a goal of serving as the world's leading center for study of ancient Near Eastern civilizations.

WEBSITES

Because of the changing nature of Internet links, Rosen Publishing has developed an online list of websites related to the subject of this book. This site is updated regularly. Please use this link to access the list:

http://www.rosenlinks.com/SRFAC/mcult

FOR FURTHER READING

Bryson, Bernarda. *Gilgamesh*. Sacramento, CA: Pied Piper Press, 2012.

Doeden, Matt. *Tools and Treasures of Ancient Mesopotamia*. Minneapolis, MN: Lerner Publishing Group, 2014.

Feinstein, Stephen. *Discovering Ancient Mesopotamia* (Discover Ancient Civilizations). Berkeley Heights, NJ: Enslow Publishers, 2014.

Head, Tom. *Ancient Mesopotamia*. Minneapolis, MN: Essential Library/ ABDO, 2014.

Hollar, Sherman, ed. *Mesopotamia* (Ancient Civilizations). New York, NY: Britannica Educational Publishing/Rosen Publishing, 2011.

Lassieur, Allison. *Ancient Mesopotamia*. New York, NY: Children's Press, 2012.

Lockwood, Gary. *The Epic of Gilgamesh: The Storyteller's Version*. Lumenarts, 2013. Audiobook.

Nardo, Don. *Mesopotamia* (Exploring the Ancient World). North Mankato, MN: Compass Point, 2012.

Oakes, Lorna. *Hands-On History Mesopotamia*. Leicester, England: Armadillo, 2013.

Wood, Alix. *Uncovering the Culture of Ancient Mesopotamia* (Archaeology and Ancient Cultures). New York, NY: Powerkids Press, 2016.

BIBLIOGRAPHY

Ascalone, Enrico. *Mesopotamia*. Trans. by Rosanna M. Gianmmanco Frongia. Berkeley, CA: University of California Press, 2005.

Bertman, Stephen. *Handbook to Life in Ancient Mesopotamia*. New York, NY: Facts On File, 2003.

Bottero, Jean. *Mesopotamia: Writing, Reasoning, and the Gods*. Trans. by Zainab Bahrani and Marc Van De Mieroop. Chicago and London: University of Chicago Press, 1992.

Delaporte, L. *Mesopotamia: The Babylonian and Assyrian Civilization*. Trans. by V. Gordon Childe. New York, NY: Barnes & Noble, 1925, reprinted 1970.

Draffkorn Kilmer, Anne. "The Musical Instruments from Ur and Ancient Mesopotamian Music." *Expedition*, Vol. 40, No. 2, 1998, pp. 12–19 (http://www.penn.museum/documents/publications/expedition/PDFs/40-2/The%20Musical1.pdf).

Mirelman, Sam. "New Developments in the Social History of Music and Musicians in Ancient Iraq, Syria, and Turkey." *Yearbook for Traditional Music*, Vol. 41, 2009, pp. 12–22.

Nemet-Nejat, Karen Rhea. *Daily Life in Ancient Mesopotamia*. Peabody, MA: Hendrickson, 1998.

Oppenheim, A. Leo. *Ancient Mesopotamia: Portrait of a Dead Civilization*. Chicago and London: University of Chicago Press, 1964, 1977.

West, M. L. "Akkadian Poetry: Metre and Performance." *Iraq*, Vol. 59, 1997, pp. 175–187.

INDEX

ABOUT THE AUTHOR

Barbara Krasner is the author of more than fourteen books for young readers. She holds an MFA in Writing for Children and Young Adults from the Vermont College of Fine Arts and teaches creative writing and children's literature in New Jersey. She first became interested in the ancient world in the fourth grade.

PHOTO CREDITS